Co

C000212986

Walk
1. Chelmorton
2. Solomon's Temple
3. Fernilee Reservoir & Goyt V
4. Two Tors Walk
5. The Six Hills Perimeter Walk   5.6   9   3
6. Chee Dale & Blackwell Circular   5.9   9.5   3
7. Goyt's Moss & Wild Moor   6.2   10   3-4
8. Harpur Hill   7   11.2   4
9. Stanley Moor & Axe Edge   8   12.9   5

Walking times shown are approximate and depend on fitness, weight of rucksack, weather, conditions underfoot and height climbed.

Level of Difficulty **1** = Easy, **3** = Moderate, **6** = Hard
All walks are shown on O.S. Explorer map No.OL24 The Peak District – White Peak Area.
Every effort has been made to ascertain the accuracy of the walks described, the description of a route or track is not necessarily a right of way.

Some abbreviations have been used in the text to shorten it and make it more concise: -
PF = Public Footpath   RT = Right   LT = Left   FB = Footbridge
CP = Car Park   m = metres   km = kilometres   °M = magnetic
RD = Road

Walkers are strongly advised to have the appropriate clothing and footwear for these walks.
- Boots/walking shoes.
- Waterproof Jacket.
- Over trousers.
- Small Rucksack for food, drinks and spare clothing.
- Hat & Gloves.
- Compass & map.

ISBN 978-1-903568-50-7

Walk 1 Chelmorton   **Distance** 3.7 miles/6 km
Start GR. 115702 Park near the church and pub in Chelmorton.
Walk Time 1 hr 30 mins
Terrain Generally a flat walk, with one steep descent into Deep Dale. Good views and easy walking with a nice refreshment stop at the start/finish in Chelmorton.

Start at the junction of Church Lane (1) about 200m down the hill from The Church Inn pub in Chelmorton. Walk along a track by some houses beside a PF sign, opposite the junction and Church Lane sign. Continue on this track, passing Shepley Farm off on your RT.

Cross a cattle grid to emerge on the A5270 RD. Opposite there are two PF, take the LT one signed Midshires Way. Continue on this track until you see a marker post on your RT and a short track off to your LT. This is about 200m before you come to a ruined building, which you should see, ahead on the main track.

Turn LT on this track for about 40m then look for an opening over the stone wall on the RT into a field. Cross five fields diagonally RT over steps in the stone walls, heading in the direction of a caravan site in the distance.

On the top of the ravine, cross a stile then descend steeply on a narrow winding path into the ravine at Deep Dale (2). Once on the bottom, turn LT to walk on a flat path between the steep hillsides of the ravine. Continue to where the ravine splits into Back Dale and Horseshoe Dale, soon after a stile and signboard.

Take the LT fork along Horseshoe Dale (3) and continue for 1km to emerge on the A5270 RD. At the main RD, turn LT, walking for 220m to a PF on the LT. Cross steps over the wall and walk to the LT of a broken wall in front of you (4). Cross steps again at the far side then walk diagonally RT to the far corner of the field. Cross steps to emerge on the A5270 RD.

Emerging on the RD, turn LT for 100m then cross to walk between two stone walls for 350m. When you emerge in a field, bear diagonally LT to the far corner (5) and through a farm gate. Walk along the narrow path between the two stone walls, passing a small barn. When you reach a minor RD, cross it and continue a further 150m to a bridleway track, turning RT along it back into Chelmorton.

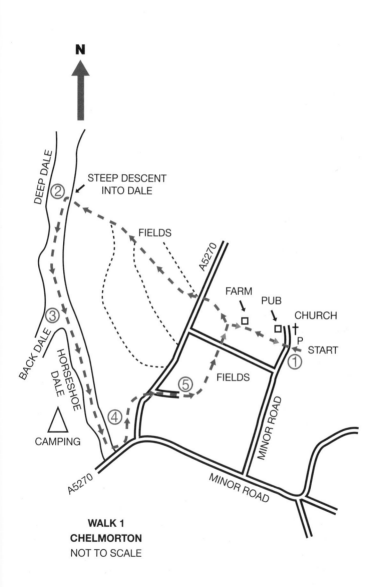

N

DEEP DALE

STEEP DESCENT
INTO DALE

②

FIELDS

A5270

FARM

PUB

CHURCH

†

P

START

①

BACK DALE

③

HORSESHOE
DALE

⑤

FIELDS

④

MINOR ROAD

CAMPING

A5270

MINOR ROAD

WALK 1
CHELMORTON
NOT TO SCALE

Walk 2 Solomon's Temple   **Distance** 4.3 miles/7 km
Start GR. 043718 Main RD at entrance to Grin Low & Buxton
Country Park. Ladmanlow.
Time 2 hrs 20 mins
Terrain A few short ascents/descents but not too demanding. Very
good views, especially from the temple and generally a nice walk.

Walk along the access RD (1) into the country park and caravan
site. Do not turn LT into the caravan park, but turn RT into
Derbyshire Council's CP. Walk to the far end of the park and stay on
the path which winds round and up over a grassed area to Solomon's
Temple (2) which you should see ahead on high ground. There are
good views from here.

After viewing the temple, walk from the temple entrance door,
downhill on a path towards the wood. Follow the path through and
down to sports pitches at the lower side (3). Cross between the
pitches to a path going LT to RT at the far side.

Turn RT and walk to the open area with a row of houses at the far
side. On reaching the row of houses, turn RT and continue on the
wide tarmac track until you reach the riding stables at the far end.
Turn RT at the stables and walk around the buildings (4) and practice
ring to the far side, following the yellow arrows. Ascend the stony
track by the side of the wood on your LT.

Go through a gate at the top and cross the field then go through an
opening at the far side and descend another field to a farm access
track. Turn RT on the track then LT off the track further along to
a PF sign on lower ground. Cross the stile there onto the RD (5),
and walk LT on the RD, descending to a PF sign and stile by a farm
entrance on the opposite side.

Walk on the access track, which ascends the hillside to the farm you
see at the top of the hill (6). Follow directions around the RT of the
farm and pick up an access track on the far side of the farm. Stay
on this track for 1.1km as it winds around the fields and past the
reservoir back to where you started at Ladmanlow.

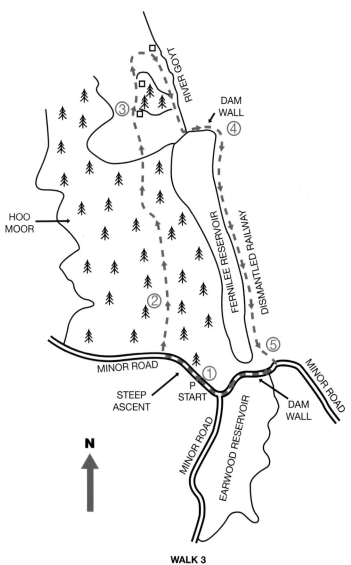

RIVER GOYT

DAM WALL
④

③

HOO
MOOR

FERNILEE RESERVOIR

DISMANTLED RAILWAY

②

⑤

MINOR ROAD

①

STEEP
ASCENT

P
START

MINOR ROAD

DAM
WALL

MINOR ROAD

N

EARWOOD RESERVOIR

WALK 3
FERNILEE RESERVOIR
NOT TO SCALE

Walk 4 Two Tors Walk   **Distance** 5.1 miles/8.2 km
Start GR. 995767 Park in Pym Chair CP near junction.
Walk Time 2hrs
Terrain An easy walk over Cats Tor to Shinning Tor, with excellent views, followed by a descent then an undulating walk along the valley below the tors, back to the CP. A short steep ascent of 1km at the finish.

From the RD junction (1) near Pym Chair CP turn LT, and walk 150m to the bend in the RD, which leads to Fernilee Reservoir. Look for a sign on the RT pointing to Shining Tor, and go through a small gate there. Ascend the grass path going up the hillside, keeping the stone wall to your RT.

Continue over Cats Tor (2), mostly on a slabbed path and straight on to the 'trig' point on the summit of Shining Tor (3). There are excellent views all the way from the start to here.

Retrace your steps back 150m to a PF sign, and turn LT to descend the hillside on the grass and peat path. As you start to ascend slightly, you come to a stile (4). DO NOT cross, but turn RT to walk on a slight descent on a narrow worn grass path down the valley. Cross another two stiles on your way down.

At the bottom of the valley, known as Thursbitch, you come to two stiles with a small ruined building at the far side. Cross the RT stile, and follow a general bearing from the stile of 343°M to Howlersknow Farm, on a path leading over another stile a short distance away. Your route now leads over a series of fields as you ascend slowly (5). The feint grass path bears LT as you walk along by a stone wall, then descend to Howlersknow Farm.

Follow the feint path to the RT of the farm then straight on to emerge on the minor RD (6). Turn RT on the RD and ascend for 1km to the junction and CP at the top where you started from.

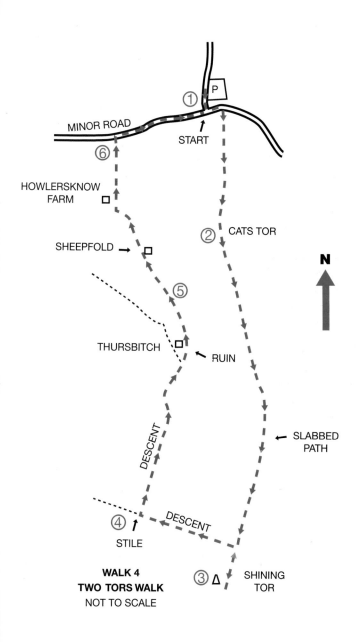

P

① START

MINOR ROAD

⑥

HOWLERSKNOW
FARM

SHEEPFOLD →

② CATS TOR

N

⑤

THURSBITCH

← RUIN

DESCENT

SLABBED
PATH →

DESCENT

④

STILE

③ △   SHINING
TOR

WALK 4
TWO TORS WALK
NOT TO SCALE

Walk 5 The Six Hills Perimeter Walk   **Distance** 5.6 miles/9 km
Start GR. 090671 Park in Earl Sterndale Village.
Walk Time 3 hrs
Terrain An undulating but very nice walk which circles five hills. Not too strenuous but with several short steep ascents.

Walking from the village, head northwest back to the main RD at the B5053 300m away (1). Cross it and ascend the minor RD past Hatch-Away for 650m to a gate on your LT leading onto a farm access track (2). Continue a short distance to a stile on the RT into a field. Cross, then head LT to the top of the hillside.

Go through a farm gate by a PF sign and cross the centre of the next field following the arrows. Continue to the far side and descend to the stile leading onto the RD in Dowel Dale (3). Ascend the RD up Dowel Dale ravine and continue on the RD past Owl Hole trees on the bend and the entrance to Greensides Farm on the RT.

Cross two cattle grids then at the next bend in the RD (4), turn off LT on a PF up an access track towards Stoop Farm. Cross a cattle grid at the top then follow a PF sign to Booth Farm. Cross the hillside and descend to a wire fence and gate in the far lower LT corner. Cross and walk on the access track round to Booth Farm.

Nearing Booth Farm, keep LT and pass the farm (5), walking on a track around the hillside, with good views down the valley. Stay on this descending track to pass a house and eventually emerge near the bottom of the valley. Turn RT to go through a small metal gate at the bottom then cross the FB over the stream and ascend a field following the feint path.

Emerging on the minor RD (6), descend LT to Hollinsclough and the village green. Turn LT near the telephone box and walk along the minor RD for 450m then at a fork, bear RT on a track. Cross a stile by a farm gate in the direction of the distinctive pointed hill. Stay on the track and go over a FB and emerge on a minor RD (7).

Cross the RD and walk around Parkhouse Hill on a narrow track. Go through a small gate, emerging in a field with a farm ahead. Bear RT here, descending to a farm gate at the bottom of the field. Cross the RD and through another gate to ascend the hillside (8) to steps over the stone wall. Cross and walk over the field and through a farm gate at the far side towards the corner of a stone wall. Descend the field diagonally RT to an opening at the side of a farm gate leading back into Earl Sterndale.

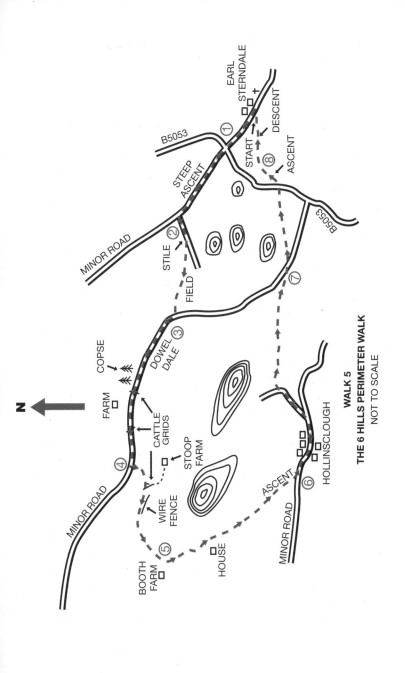

N

WALK 5

THE 6 HILLS PERIMETER WALK

NOT TO SCALE

EARL STERNDALE

START

DESCENT

ASCENT

B5053

B5053

STEEP ASCENT

MINOR ROAD

STILE

FIELD

DOWEL DALE

COPSE

FARM

CATTLE GRIDS

STOOP FARM

MINOR ROAD

WIRE FENCE

BOOTH FARM

HOUSE

ASCENT

MINOR ROAD

HOLLINSCLOUGH

① ② ③ ④ ⑤ ⑥ ⑦ ⑧

Walk 6 Chee Dale & Blackwell Circular   **Distance** 5.9 miles/9.5 km
Start GR. 132714 Park and start from The Waterloo pub on the A6.
Walk Time 3 hrs 10 mins
Terrain A very nice walk through Chee Dale to Miller's Dale along
the ravine bottom. Good and interesting scenery. Path may be muddy
and rocks underfoot slippery in wet weather. Not too strenuous apart
from the 1.4km ascent on a track near the end.

From 'The Waterloo' pub, walk up the track to the LT of it (1).
Go through a farm gate and follow it round to a wooden farm gate
and sign. Turn RT over stone steps to descend the hillside steeply to
the small wood at the bottom. Keep by the wall all the way down and
emerge on the A6 RD (2).

Turn LT on the A6 and at the far side of the wood join Senners Lane
(track). Stay on this for 700m until you meet a tarmac RD, signed
Pennine Bridleway, turn down this, back to the A6. Cross with care and
then continue at the far side for 300m to a bend in the RD (3).

Turn LT here and stay on the Pennine Bridleway track all the way
in the same direction, passing through several fields and gates.
Approaching the A6 RD, your route bends round and descends steeply
into the ravine at Chee Dale (4) going right to the bottom to join a
section of the Monsal Trail.

At the bottom of the ravine, turn RT and walk for 1.5km, passing
through several short tunnels. On reaching a dead end, follow the
sign for Miller's Dale, and turn off RT on a path, which soon divides.
Take the RT fork, which takes you over a FB. From here you walk
closely beside the River Wye for approx 1.4km on a muddy path to a
large railway bridge (5).

Turn LT and ascend stone steps at the side to emerge on the bridge at
the top. Cross the bridge and follow a PF sign LT through a narrow
opening at the far side onto a narrow path. Emerging in a field at the
top corner of woodland, turn LT to descend the field in the centre, and
cross a stile at the bottom. Ascend steeply to the B6049 RD, and turn
LT for 100m.

Cross the RD with care and turn sharp RT (6) to walk steeply up
Long Lane (track) for 1.4km to emerge on a RD. Continue to the lane
crossroads 140m along (7) then turn RT to take you back to The
Waterloo pub where you started.

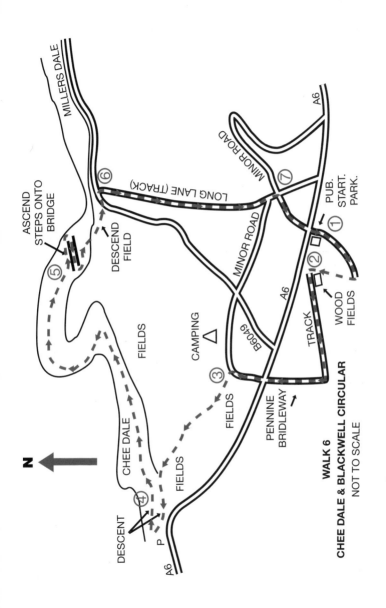

WALK 6
CHEE DALE & BLACKWELL CIRCULAR
NOT TO SCALE

Walk 7 Goyt's Moss & Wild Moor   **Distance** 6.2 miles/10 km
Start GR. 036724 In Macclesfield Old RD adjacent to Christchurch.
Walk Time 3hrs 40 mins
Terrain Some hills to descend and ascend on what can be a testing walk, with good views throughout.

Park at the top end of the lane, and walk up to the signpost on the RT by the wood (1). The lane turns into a track on the top end. Cross a stile, following the sign towards Lamaload and Shining Tor. Ascend alongside the wall by the wood then at the end of the stone wall, bear RT and ascend over the field diagonally to a gate at the top corner of the field (2).

Cross over the moor on the path then descend a long narrow winding path for 1.8km to a FB over the stream (3), near a minor RD. DO NOT cross the FB but bear RT and follow the sign towards Goytsclough Quarry, on a narrow path which ascends over the hillside.

You come to a broken stone wall, 1.2km from the FB. Turn RT here and ascend the hillside steeply, keeping the wall just to your LT. Ascend for 500m until you see a distinct track off to your LT (4). Take a bearing of 18°M here, and follow a feint path descending over the moor towards the RT of Errwood Reservoir.

Descend to a stone wall ahead then turn RT for 100m along side it, then LT for 250m, keeping the wall just to your LT. Then cross Wildmoorstone Brook. Look for a path 50m past the far side of the brook (5), and ascend the valley on this path on a general bearing of 123°M from the paths crossroad.

Near the head of the valley, you come to several signposts and a tunnel that is now blocked. Follow the sign near the tunnel LT to Buxton & Bishops Lane. This takes you over the moor and to the corner of a wood (6). Cross a ladder stile and down through Beet Wood.

You pass some houses and a large pond on your RT, by the RD. As you pass the posts and gatehouse of Plex Lodge, turn RT to ascend the access lane to Plex Farm (7). Continue up the lane to Tunnel Farm then turn LT over a stile and along the dismantled railway (8) for 1km to emerge back at the top of Macclesfield Old Road. Turn LT to walk back down the lane to your starting point.

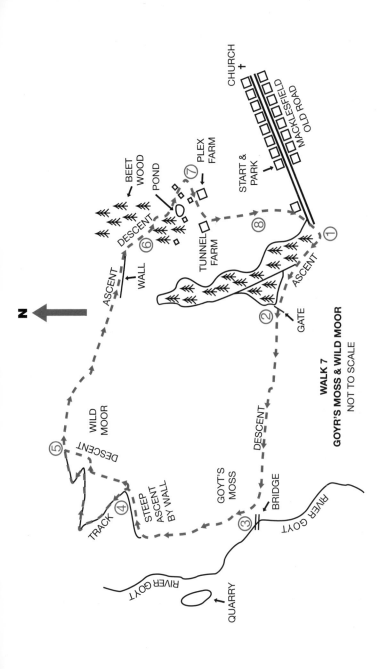

N

CHURCH

MACKLESFIELD OLD ROAD

START & PARK

① ASCENT

BEET WOOD

POND

⑦ PLEX FARM

DESCENT ⑥

WALL ASCENT

TUNNEL FARM

⑧

② GATE

DESCENT

GOYT'S MOSS

WILD MOOR

DESCENT

⑤

TRACK ④

STEEP ASCENT BY WALL

③ BRIDGE

RIVER GOYT

QUARRY

RIVER GOYT

WALK 7
GOYR'S MOSS & WILD MOOR
NOT TO SCALE

Walk 8 Harpur Hill Round   **Distance** 7 miles/11.2 km
Start GR. 060725 Park in White Knowle RD but start in Fern RD.
Walk Time 3hrs 20 mins
Terrain Mostly flat but scenic walk with only short ascents/descents.
Start at the entrance to Fern RD (1), just off the A515, 500m from the
hospital. Walk along Fern RD, keeping a row of houses just off to your LT.
Cross a cattle grid and continue on the wide tarmac track (2) until you reach the
riding stables at the far end. Turn RT here and walk around the buildings and
practice ring to the far side, following the yellow arrows. Ascend the stony track
by the side of the wood on your LT.

Go through a gate at the top and cross the field then go through an
opening at the far side and descend another field to a farm access track.
Turn RT on the track then LT off the track further along to a PF sign on
lower ground. Cross the stile and walk LT on the RD (3), descending then
ascending to a junction by Parks Inn.

Turn RT and continue past a church on your LT. Pass a college on your LT
then before you start to descend the hill, turn RT along Haslin RD (4) past some
houses. Go through a small gate in the corner at the far end of the RD. Walk on
grass to the far end and through a farm gate towards a railway bridge. At the
small bridge, ascend onto the old railway track above.

Turn LT on the railway track and walk towards the wood you see further along.
Where the railway track is blocked off, follow the path onto the RD to the far
side. Continue back on the track before turning up a narrow path off RT to walk
parallel with the line (5).

You come to a bridge over a railway line on your LT. DO NOT cross it but
continue a further 200m to a stile, cross then descend a path between the wall
and a wire fence. Keep by the wall to descend then ascend to a kissing gate by a
railway arch. Go under the arch then through the kissing gate at the far side.

In the distance you will see a RD junction by the busy A515 (6). Descend the
field in a straight line; crossing a further two fields to the junction by a bookstore
(6). Emerging on the minor RD, walk to the main RD; turn LT for 100m then
RT by the side of a small wood. Turn off at the entrance onto a PF behind a
farm gate.

Descend to the lower ground at the start of the ravine, between the short hillsides
and follow it along Back Dale in the ravine. Where Back Dale meets Horseshoe
Dale (7), turn LT through a gate, to ascend steeply up the short hillside.

At the top, turn RT, walking along the top of the hillside for 250m to a gate on
the LT (8). Cross the field to go through a gate in the centre at the far side. Cross
the next large field diagonally RT, to emerge on a short access lane, leading
onto a minor RD.

Turn RT on the RD for 150m then LT through a gate into a long field (9), walking
down the LT side of the field to the far end. Go through the gate there and turn

RT along the edge of the field, heading towards a farm ahead at Cowdale.
Cross steps over the wall into Cowdale then turn RT for 30m then turn LT through
an opening in the wall into a copse. Cross another stone wall then walk behind a
farm building towards the trees you see in the distance ahead. Continue on a slight
ascent to buildings at the top to emerge on an access track (**10**).

Stay on this track following it down to a caravan site then on to the railway
viaduct. Walk under the viaduct on the higher ground then descend a path to the
A515 RD. Turn RT at the junction, walking for 500m back to where you started
the walk.

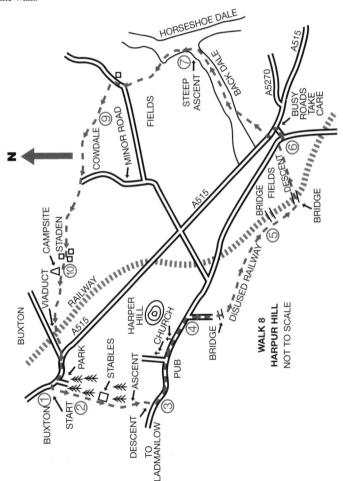

Walk 9 Stanley Moor & Axe Edge   **Distance** 8 miles/12.9 km
Start GR. 043718 Opposite the entrance to Grin Low & Buxton Country Park at Ladmanlow
Walk Time 3hrs 45 mins
Terrain A challenge which starts with an easy walk, before some steep ascents then levels out before a nice descent to the finish. Great views.

From the main RD, walk south between the houses following the PF sign through a farm gate onto a track (**1**). Keep on this track all the way past the reservoir and round to Countess Cliff Farm (**2**). As you approach the farm, look for a stile over the wall on your RT, cross then walk over fields to the lower corner. Cross into the next field by the signboard and ascend the field to the top, past two cabins.

You emerge on a track at the top and follow it RT and along the LT side of a wood. At a crossing with several PF signs, continue straight across and pass the buildings there. Keep in the same direction and go over a stile by a farm gate towards the wood. Ascend steeply and go through a kissing gate at the top onto a minor RD (**3**).

Cross the minor RD to ascend over the hillside and down the far side to a small bridge and wood on lower ground. Go through a gate then turn LT through another gate next to it. Descend a stony access track past a house and look for a small gate. Go through the gate and look for two houses below on the LT.

Cross a stile at the side of a small farm and ascend the access track through the trees then steeply up to the minor RD near Brand Top (**4**). Go through double farm gates onto the RD then turn RT for 150m to a stile on your LT, leading over the hillside. Descending now, you come to a path between two stone walls then to a minor RD. Cross, and then descend again on the access track at the far side leading to Mount Pleasant Farm.

At the bottom of the lane, look for a gate on the LT, leading up the hillside to Wallnook (house). Follow the sign to the main RD and cross with care, onto an ascending track to the shooting club (**5**). Pass the house at the top and stay on the winding track to the next LT hand bend. DO NOT follow the directions on the two posts there, but at the bend in the track (**6**), continue straight ahead on a narrow path over the grass and peat, ascending over the hillside in a northerly direction to a group of stones.

Continue on the worn path over the moor in the same direction to the minor RD (**7**). Look for the small white post at the RD and follow that track on the far side. Continue over the hillside and descend to the busy A54 RD (**8**). Turn RT and walk along the RD for 400m to a track straight ahead through a farm gate.

Stay on this track to a RT hand bend then go straight across to descend a grass hillside (**9**) back to Ladmanlow below. Continue down to the main RD then a short distance further to the minor RD on the RT, taking you back to the start 350m further along at the entrance to Grin Low Country Park.

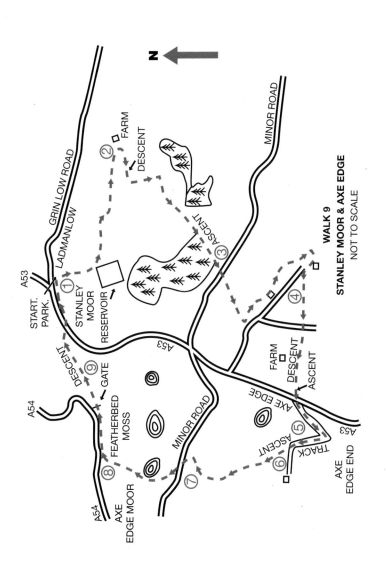

WALK 9
STANLEY MOOR & AXE EDGE
NOT TO SCALE

N

GRIN LOW ROAD
LADMANLOW
A53
START.
PARK.
STANLEY
MOOR
RESERVOIR
DESCENT
GATE
DESCENT
A54
FEATHERBED
MOSS
A54
AXE
EDGE MOOR
MINOR ROAD
A53
FARM
DESCENT
ASCENT
FARM
DESCENT
ASCENT
AXE EDGE
AXE
EDGE END
A53
TRACK
ASCENT
MINOR ROAD
ASCENT

① ② ③ ④ ⑤ ⑥ ⑦ ⑧ ⑨

Notes

Bush Theatre

HARM

by Phoebe Eclair-Powell

Opened on 17 May 2021
Bush Theatre, London

HARM

by Phoebe Eclair-Powell

Cast

Woman · **Kelly Gough**

Creative Team

Director	**Atri Banerjee**
Set and Costume Designer	**Rosanna Vize**
Lighting Designer	**Lee Curran**
Sound Designer	**Jasmin Kent Rodgman**
Prop Maker	**Liz Putland**
Movement Director	**Chi-San Howard**
Dramaturg	**Deirdre O'Halloran**
Casting Director	**Annelie Powell CDG**
Production Manager	**Jerome Reid**
Company Stage Manager	**Kala Simpson**
Assistant Stage Manager	**Hanne Schulpé**
Cover Assistant Stage Manager	**Lois Sime**

With thanks to Leanne Best, Rike Berg and Imogen Knight.

CAST

Kelly Gough | Woman

Kelly Gough is an Irish actor, based in London. Kelly's theatre credits include: *A Streetcar Named Desire* (English Touring Theatre); *Don Carlos* (ARA); *Macbeth* (Second Age); *All in the Timing* (Iris Theatre); *Big Love* (Abbey Theatre); *Falling Out of Love* (Yew Tree Theatre); *Macbecks* (Long Road Productions); *Pilgrims of the Night* (Rough Magic); *The Playboy of the Western World* (Druid Theatre); *Phaedra*, *Vinegar Tom*, *Terrorism*, *Three Sisters*, *Twelfth Night* and *The Yeats Trilogy* (Samuel Beckett Theatre). On film she has appeared in the shorts: *In PurSUEt*, *Taking Stock* and *Cry Rosa*, plus *Out of Innocence*, *Kill Comman*, *Jump* and *Belonging to Laura*. Her television credits include: *Marcella*, *Call the Midwife*, *Strike Back*, *Broadchurch* (series 3), *Class*, *The Fall* (series 2 and 3), *Country Woman*, *Vera*, *Casualty*, *Law & Order*, *Raw* (series 2–5), *Scup*, *This Is Nightlive*, *An Crisis* and *The Clinic*.

CREATIVE TEAM

Phoebe Eclair-Powell | Writer

Phoebe Eclair-Powell is a writer from south-east London, and the most recent winner of the Bruntwood Prize for her play *Shed:Exploded View*. In 2015, Phoebe's debut play, *WINK* at Theatre503, received rave reviews and four OffWestEnd nominations including Most Promising New Playwright. Her play *Fury* was runner-up for the Verity Bargate Award 2015, and subsequently won the Soho Young Writer's Award and had its run extended at Soho Theatre due to popular demand. It also received an OffWestEnd nomination for Best Play.

Atri Banerjee | Director

Atri Banerjee won The Stage Debut Award for Best Director in 2019 for his production of *Hobson's Choice* at the Royal Exchange Theatre, Manchester. Other directing credits include: *Europe* (LAMDA) and *Utopia* (Royal Exchange, Manchester). He was previously Trainee Director at the Royal Exchange, where he was Assistant/Associate Director on productions including: *West Side Story*, *The Mysteries* (also tour), *Happy Days*, *The Almighty Sometimes*, *Jubilee* (also Lyric Hammersmith) and *Our Town*. Other Assistant/Associate Director credits include: *The Nico Project* (Manchester International Festival and Melbourne International Arts Festival) and *The Son* (Kiln Theatre). He trained at Birkbeck and is currently a Resident Director at the Almeida Theatre.

Rosanna Vize | Set and Costume Designer

Rosanna Vize trained at Bristol Old Vic Theatre School as a theatre designer. She has worked regularly as an assistant to Anna Fleischle and was the resident design assistant for the RSC from September 2014 to September 2015. She was a Linbury Prize Finalist in 2013 working with English Touring Opera and is currently one of the Jerwood Young Designers. Theatre includes: *King Lear* (Shakespeare's Globe); *Hedda Gabler* (Sherman Theatre); *The Earthworks & Myth* (Royal Shakespeare Company); *The Almighty Sometimes* (Royal Exchange, Manchester); *Yous Two*, *The Phlebotomist* (Hampstead Theatre); *Henry I* (Reading Between the Lines); *Girls* (Soho Theatre, Hightide & Talawa Theatre); *FUP*, *Noye's Fludde* (Kneehigh Theatre); *Dark Land Lighthouse*, *St Joan of the Stockyards*, *A Thousand Seasons Passed*, *The Tinder Box*, *The Last Days of Mankind*, *Talon* (Bristol Old Vic); *Diary of a Madman*, *The Rise and Shine of Comrade Fiasco* (Gate Theatre); *Infinite Lives*, *Coastal Defenses* (Tobacco Factory Theatres); *Banksy: The Room in the Elephant* (Tobacco Factory Theatre and Traverse Theatre); *Edward Gant's Amazing Feats of Loneliness*, *Wicked Lady* (Bristol Old Vic Theatre School); *The Picture of John Grey* (Old Red Lion); *Measure for Measure* (Oxford School of Drama).

Lee Curran | Lighting Designer

Lee Curran is a lighting designer of theatre, dance, and opera. Lee has worked with artists and organisations such as the National Theatre, Royal Court, Hofesh Shechter, Regent's Park Open Air Theatre, Almeida Theatre, Royal Shakespeare Company, Rambert Dance Company, Donmar Warehouse, Royal Opera House, Royal Exchange, Manchester, LIFT, Boy Blue Entertainment, Young Vic, English Touring Theatre, Nederlands Dans Theater, and the Royal Danish Opera. Lee has received three Olivier nominations, for *Summer and Smoke*, *Jesus Christ Superstar* and *Constellations*. He has also received three Knight of Illumination nominations, for *Summer and Smoke*, *Jesus Christ Superstar* and *Orphée et Eurydice*.

Jasmin Kent Rodgman | Sound Designer

Jasmin Kent Rodgman is a London-born British-Malaysian artist and composer. Her music and productions have been performed across the world with partners including London Fashion Week, World Music Festival Shanghai, Edinburgh International Festival, Wilderness Festival, Roundhouse, Shoreditch Town Hall, Barbican, Oxford Playhouse and the Royal Albert Hall. Her film scores have featured at festivals such as Sundance, SXSW, Toronto International Film Festival, Kaohsiung International Film Festival and the London Short Film Festival. In 2017/18, she was a London Symphony Orchestra Jerwood Composer for the 2018 LSO season, and in 2018/19 she was a British Council and PRS Foundation Musician in Residence, in Lanzhou, North-West China. In 2019/20 she received awards from Help Musicians UK, PRS Foundation, Women Make Music and Sound & Music to support her debut EP; site-specific music installation, *Triptych*; and Instagram opera *Nineteen Ways of Looking*.

Chi-San Howard | Movement Director

Chi-San Howard's movement work includes: *Living Newspaper Edition 5* (Royal Court); *Sunnymeade Court* (Defibrillator Theatre); *The Effect* (English Theatre Frankfurt); *The Sugar Syndrome* (Orange Tree Theatre); *Oor Wullie* (Dundee Rep/national tour); *Variations* (NT Connections); *Skellig* (Nottingham Playhouse); *Under the Umbrella* (Belgrade Theatre/Yellow Earth/Tamasha); *Describe the Night* (Hampstead Theatre); *Fairytale Revolution*, *In Event of Moone Disaster* (Theatre503); *Cosmic Scallies* (Royal Exchange, Manchester/Graeae); *Moth* (Hope Mill Theatre); *The Curious Case of Benjamin Button*, *Scarlet*, *The Tempest* (Southwark Playhouse); *Adding Machine: A Musical* (Finborough Theatre). Film includes: *Hurt* by Paradise (Sulk Youth Films); music videos 'Pretending' by Orla Gartland and 'I Wonder Why' by Joesef (Spindle Productions); *Birds of Paradise* (Pemberton Films).

Deirdre O'Halloran | Dramaturg

Deirdre O'Halloran is the Literary Manager at the Bush Theatre, working to identify and build relationships with new writers, commission new work and guide plays to the stage. At the Bush she's dramaturged plays including: Olivier Award-winner *Baby Reindeer* by Richard Gadd, *The High Table* by Temi Wilkey and *An Adventure* by Vinay Patel. Deirdre was previously Literary Associate at Soho Theatre, where she worked as a dramaturg on plays including: *Girls* by Theresa Ikoko and *Fury* by Phoebe Eclair-Powell. She led on Soho Theatre's Writers' Lab programme and the biennial Verity Bargate Award. As a freelancer, Deirdre has also been a reader for Out of Joint, Sonia Friedman Productions and Papatango.

Annelie Powell CDG | Casting

Annelie Powell CDG is a casting director for stage and screen. She was Head of Casting for Nuffield Theatres Southampton from 2017 to 2020, and has also worked prolifically on a freelance basis. Recent credits include: *Wendy and Peter Pan* (Leeds Playhouse); *What's New, Pussycat?* (Birmingham Rep); *The House of Shades* (Almeida Theatre); *Romeo & Juliet* (Regent's Park Open Air Theatre); *Faustus: That Damned Woman* (Lyric Hammersmith); *Vassa* (Almeida Theatre); *Pavilion* (Theatr Clwyd); *The Pope* (Royal & Derngate Northampton); *The Weatherman* (Park Theatre); *Wolfie* (Theatre503); *Cougar* (Orange Tree Theatre); *Don Quixote* (RSC, West End); *Othello* (English Touring Theatre); *Describe the Night* (Hampstead Theatre); *Hamlet*, *King Lear* , *Imperium*, *Myth*, *The Rover*, *Seven Acts of Mercy*, *Two Noble Kinsman*, *Oppenheimer* (co-casting), *The Shoemaker's Holiday* (co-casting), *Faustus* (co-casting) (Royal Shakespeare Company). She also works extensively in television and film working with companies such as the BBC, Netflix, Warnerbros, SKY and Viacom.

Bush
Theatre
We make theatre
for London. Now.

The Bush is a world-famous home for new plays and an internationally renowned champion of playwrights. We discover, nurture and produce the best new writers from the widest range of backgrounds from our home in a distinctive corner of west London.

The Bush has won over 100 awards and developed an enviable reputation for touring its acclaimed productions nationally and internationally.

We are excited by exceptional new voices, stories and perspectives – particularly those with contemporary bite which reflect the vibrancy of British culture now.

Located in the newly renovated old library on Uxbridge Road in the heart of Shepherd's Bush, the theatre houses two performance spaces, a rehearsal room and the lively Library Bar.

bushtheatre.co.uk

Bush Theatre

Artistic Director	Lynette Linton
Executive Director	Lauren Clancy
Literary Assistant	Gift Ajimokun
Associate Director	Daniel Bailey
Senior Technician	Francis Botu
Head of Marketing	Beatrice Burrows
Producer	Jessica Campbell
Digital Marketing Officer	Shannon Clarke
Development Officer	Florence Collenette
Head of Development	Ruth Davey
Finance Assistant	Lauren Francis
Community Assistant	Katie Greenall
Head of Finance	Neil Harris
Digital Producer	Cheryl Jordan Osei
Assistant Venue Operations Manager	Tim McNiven
Literary Manager	Deirdre O'Halloran
Associate Producer	Oscar Owen
Theatre Administrator and Event Producer	Jessica Pentney
Press Manager	Martin Shippen
Community Producer	Holly Smith
Technical Manager	Ian Taylor
Marketing and Ticketing Officer	Ed Theakston
Development Assistant	Eleanor Tindall
General Manager	Angela Wachner
Venue Operations Manager	Barbara Zemper

Duty Managers
Ilaria Ciardelli, Jack Cook, Ryan Cottee, Isabele Hernandez, Marissa McKinnon and Eljai Morais

Bar Supervisors
David Bolwell, Nieta Irons, Chantal-Carine Neckles, Sophie Romer, Sidsel Rostrup, Melissa Stephen and Rafael Uzcategui

Box Office, Bar & Front of House Team
Roxane Cabassut, Ayesha Charles, Ewa Dina, Lydia Feerick, Joshua Glenister, Kelsey Gordon, Matias Hailu, Olivia Hanrahan-Barnes, Judd Launder, Munaye Lichtenstein, Sara Malik, Matilda McNair, Jennefer O'Garrow, Emily Orme, Max Partridge, Charlie Phillips, Jasmine Prince, Humaira Wadiwala, Robin Wilks, Charlie Wood

Board of Trustees:
Simon Johnson (Chair), Mark Dakin, Simon Dowson-Collins, Nia Janis, Nike Jonah, Lynette Linton, Kathryn Marten, Rajiv Parkash, Stephen Pidcock and Catherine Score

Bush Theatre, 7 Uxbridge Road, London W12 8LJ
Box Office: 020 8743 5050 | Administration: 020 8743 3584
Email: info@bushtheatre.co.uk
bushtheatre.co.uk

Alternative Theatre Company Ltd
The Bush Theatre is a Registered Charity and a company limited by guarantee.
Registered in England no. 1221968 Charity no. 270080

THANK YOU

The Bush Theatre would like to thank all its supporters whose valuable contributions have helped us to create a platform for our future and to promote the highest quality new writing, develop the next generation of creative talent, lead innovative community engagement work and champion diversity.

MAJOR DONORS
Gianni & Michael Alen-Buckley
Charles Holloway
Georgia Oetker
Susie Simkins
Jack Thorne

LONE STARS
Gianni Alen-Buckley
Michael Alen-Buckley
Jacqui Bull
Rafael & Anne-Helene Biosse Duplan
Charles Holloway
Priscilla John
Rosemary Morgan
Georgia Oetker
Susie Simkins
Jack Thorne

HANDFUL OF STARS
Charlie Bigham
Judy Bollinger
Clive & Helena Butler
Clyde Cooper
Sue Fletcher
Joanna Kennedy
Simon & Katherine Johnson
Garry Lawrence
V&F Lukey
Anthony Marraccino
Aditya Mittal
Robert Ledger & Sally Moulsdale
Clare Rich
Lesley Hill & Russ Shaw
Kit and Anthony Van Tulleken

RISING STARS
Holly & Bruno Albutt
Naluwembe Binaisa
David Brooks
Catharine Browne
Matthew Byam Shaw
Philip Cameron & Richard Smith
Esperanza Cerdan
Grace Chan
Penelope Christie
Lauren Clancy
Tim & Andrea Clark
Sarah Clarke
Claude & Susie Cochin de Billy
Susie Cuff
Matthew Cushen
Philippa Dolphin
Sarah Edwards
Jack Gordon & Kate Lacy
Hugh & Sarah Grootenhuis
Thea Guest
Nick Hern
Patrick Harrison
Fiona l'Anson
Davina & Malcolm Judelson
Lynette Linton
Miggy Littlejohns
Judith Mellor
Caro Millington
Danny Morrison
Dan & Laurie Mucha
Rajiv Parkash
Mark & Anne Paterson
Renske Mann & Marion Mathews
Brian Smith
Joe Tinston & Amelia Knott
Peter Tausig
Jan Topham
Guy Vincent & Sarah Mitchell

CORPORATE SPONSORS
Biznography
Dorsett Shepherds Bush
Jamie Lloyd Company
Studio Doug
U+I
Wychwood Media

TRUSTS AND FOUNDATIONS
29th May 1961 Charitable Trust
Christina Smith Foundation
Cockayne Foundation - Grants for the Arts
The Daisy Trust
Esmee Fairbairn
Foyle Foundation
Garfield Weston Foundation
The Harold Hyam Wingate Foundation
John Lyon's Charity
Leche Trust
The Martin Bowley Charitable Trust
One anonymous donor
Orange Tree Trust
Royal Victoria Hall Foundation
The Teale Charitable Trust
Tudor Trust
Victoria Wood Foundation

Supported by
ARTS COUNCIL ENGLAND

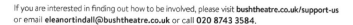

If you are interested in finding out how to be involved, please visit **bushtheatre.co.uk/support-us** or email **eleanortindall@bushtheatre.co.uk** or call **020 8743 3584.**

HARM

Phoebe Eclair-Powell

Thanks

My first and foremost thanks must go to *The Artist's Way* by
Julia Cameron – because this play came out of the exercises and
creative inspiration contained in that genius book. I'm very
grateful to Jess Edwards for making me buy it!

My next thanks must go to Lynette Linton who believed in this
idea from the seed and steered me towards the looking-glass
world of Instagram and who gave the play its first theatrical
outing. I am forever grateful. To Deirdre O'Halloran, the
dramaturg of dreams. I owe you everything, Dee. And, of
course, to Daniel Bailey who always kept supporting, helping,
advising with kindness. To the lovely Jess Campbell – what a
joy you are. My biggest thanks to Lauren and the whole Bush
Theatre team who are just insanely lovely and kind and who
have been superstars.

To the creative team behind *Harm* in its many iterations. To the
Angelica Films crew who made it into a film in three weeks –
you are my heroes. To Monika Davies, Imogen Knight, Andrew
Fettis, Mellissa Munslow, Emily Farrell, Alex Daniels, Amir
Aal, Laurence Johnson, Bill Rae Smith, Ana Vilar, Shane
Gravestock. The happiest three days. To the stage managers
who are always the real heroes: Rike Berg, Crystal Gayle,
Hanne Schulpé and Kala Simpson.

To the beautifully talented Rosie Vize, Chi-San Howard, Lee
Curran and Jasmin Kent Rodgman. And a big shout-out to Liz
Putland the prop-maker extraordinaire.

To my two WOMANS, Leanne Best you really are a true
phenomenon, special soul, and an extremely magical word
witch. And Kelly Gough – just wow, what tenacity of thought
and spirit. I consider myself extremely lucky to have been in the
same room as you both. Thank you to the moon and back.

To my agent, Ikenna Obiekwe, as ever. And to the generous minds of Owen Horsley and Jon Brittain. And the ever-patient and brill team at Nick Hern – thank you!

And finally, to Atri Banerjee. You are so talented and kind and good it hurts. You are my white rabbit. Love.

P. E-P.

Characters

WOMAN

This text went to press before the end of rehearsals and so may differ slightly from the play as performed.

I am thirty-nine years old

There are these pigeons that have sex on my windowsill and
I watch them a little too long sometimes. Trying to remember
that feeling – coo – coo.

Breakfast is a Ryvita, not because I'm on a diet but because
that's what's in my cupboard, that and a tin of tuna, which is
just frankly antisocial of a morning. You might as well eat a can
of Whiskas.

The bus to work is busy – heaving – and I try to count like the
app told me to count as I scroll through photos of other people's
weekends on Instagram – wedding in a field – wild swimming
in Shadwell – sourdough – kitten – kitten – heavily filtered
selfie – kitten… and breathe…

I tell the WhatsApp group about the rush to work and no one
replies – which is fine because they're mostly all teachers and
they've been at work for two hours already – dick'eads.

The office is your classic estate agent on a mini high street –
next to other estate agents that are posher or crapper – and
everything is roughly overpriced or quite frankly a brothel with
damp. And we sit and we type and we tell people that this area
is becoming very sought after – transport links et cetera et
cetera and then we go home. On repeat. And sometimes,
sometimes there is a birthday card to sign. My boss Barry –
doesn't even tell me off for the lateness today. He likes me.
I once gave him a handjob at a Christmas party because well…
It was Christmas and it's served me really well ever since.
Probably more than the degree.

Morning Barry –

See Barry does this thing where he winks and whistles a lot
when he's about to share something exciting, sort of like a party

trick but shit – and he's doing it for ages today – like really going for it, wink whistle wink whistle.

Until finally he parks his sweaty arse on the corner of my desk and says – got a big fucker – got a two-point-one mill – and I think okay… okay Barry good for you – and he says but I'm at the agency expo in Brussels – so it's all yours –

All fucking yours…

He leans in and says pay me back later.

Wink whistle wink whistle.

And he sends me the details –

And the pictures are… beautiful – the house for sale is a dream house, like a drawing of a house, like a little kid's idea of the perfect house, there's a swing and a porch and a rockery and a tasteful little balcony and these rose bushes and I am starting to fall in love with this house…

Thing is – it's in West Norwood – and before you sniff, Norwood is becoming the new sort of Forest Hill which is like the boring cousin of Brockley – which is the new Nunhead, which itself is like a mini Camberwell – which is the sadder sister of Peckham. Basically it's leafy and full of smug middle-class couples who care about the environment so open up plastic-free shops but have multiple kids and the average plan on a Saturday night is to eat a very large vegan pizza – and that's it.

I invite Barry for a drink after work to say thank you – but he has fucking football

Please.

I could do that, there's an all-women's team near me called Bend It Like Peckham, fucking fabulous, they stride round Peckham Rye in tiny shorts and large thighs and they're crap at football, but I watch them having a post-match drink at the local pub, me and my phone, and they look muddy and ruddy and really, really… happy.

When I get home – to my tiny ground-floor flat off the Old Kent Road – I spend all night watching YouTube videos of car accidents. I check up on Reddit, best cheese, worst cheese, foot cheese, people who look like cheese, knob cheese... I am thirty-nine years old.

I send a picture of a wheel of cheese with Jesus's face on it to my WhatsApp group... and no one replies. I scroll through and realise that I am the only one to have posted anything for the past six weeks. Which is fine... because everyone is very, very busy. I'm busy. We all have very busy lives.

I'm bored so I text Barry
How was football did you lose?
Two little blue ticks
He doesn't reply

Whatever.

Sometimes... sometimes I don't brush my teeth before bed and I enjoy the fact that there's no one there to tell me I smell.

Alice

I show people the house. The beautiful two-point-one-million-pound house.

I stand on the porch by the wisteria which is so very, very in and show shiny beautiful couples around the shiny beautiful house and I smile and they smile – and when I tell them the asking price… they stop smiling – and leave…

But not her – no, she's special. I know it the second she closes the car door of her expensively shit vintage Mini – it's yours.

She glides towards me – with her just-fashionable maxi dress and her actual leather jacket – she's beautiful in a natural, very natural, oh-so-very-engineered-to-be-natural way and she glows like her name might be Honeysuckle, or Tuppence… I bet she owns Kilner Jars.
And I want her immediately.
To suffer something unfortunate.
To be friends with me
Both
I don't know
I'm shaking her hand
I'm Alice she says

I forget to tell her my name.

The house is a warren of tall ceiling after even taller ceiling and she is in love. I watch her face beam as she gets out her phone – and videos herself walking though it – I have never seen someone do this – talking to the camera.
I clear my throat
– *oh I'll have to do it again* she sighs.
She looks at my face – my confused face
– *I do this for a living* –
She's an influencer – on Instagram, a mix of lifestyle, fashion and travel.
Her smile I realise now is whiter than mine. She's wearing two kinds of beige eyeshadow.

She nods to my phone and gestures – *here* – and just like that
I'm following her – and her little counter goes up. One-point-
one million.
Million.
It's strange but I immediately think she's famous – even though
she's not Madonna, or even someone from the telly – she's just
standing there in front of me and
I follow her now.
Through the house
Even though it should be the other way around.

Later – I go to hand her the specifications but she whips her
phone out and rings her partner – and she puts on this slightly
higher little girl's voice, *I know it's a lot but it's perfect you
don't understand how fucking perfect it is Daniel… Daniel…
We'll take it* she smiles – and she walks out of the house and
into her Mini and drives away…

Alice.

The offer

Barry FaceTimes me from Brussels whilst eating an extremely large pretzel, crumbs everywhere – have I sold it yet? I pretend I can't hear him and hang up.

I get an email from Alice – it has lots of exclamation marks – *they are sooooo excited, let them know what the owners think of the offer yeah –*

I look at her Instagram – she has posted a picture of her crossing her fingers:

waiting for good news lol send me your lucky thoughts and vibes #Prayers

I comment underneath, hope I can provide it lol. She hearts my comment. I get a hundred and twenty-two new followers.

End of day she rings me – *any news* – I tell her nothing yet – so sorry...

The reason why is that I haven't put the offer in.

That night I scroll through to her very first post. She is holding a man's hand and jumping through waves. She is golden tanned and thinner. I look at my first post. A cup of coffee... a biscuit on the side.

I still don't put the offer in.

I watch documentaries about serial killers on Netflix until I wake up in a pool of my own sweat and a message from Alice – *hopefully today yeah?*

After a few hours she rings me –

I tell her there is a lot of competition on the house – that the sellers are taking their time, an old couple who live in France now – it will be fine, I say. I told them how much you wanted it – that you were the best buyers of the lot.

I lie and I lie, and I lie.

I offer to go over to hers with some brochures, so I can show her what else we have on offer –

She sighs a sad little *okay* back –

I borrow the company car – even though Barry has warned me twice not to take it out of office hours. Fuck off Barry suck my tits in your dreams.

Her flat is in that bit between East Dulwich and Peckham Rye, pink door, trendy wallpaper. There is a hammock in the sitting room because – why not – and everything looks like it came from MADE.com. There *are* jars – filled with different gluten-free pastas – and a pizza oven – *I got that free* she coos – *and here, here is my awards shelf*. She has won awards. For her Instagram, her YouTube... her life. She has won awards for the way her fingernails never seem to chip.

She flicks through the brochures and shrugs a bit, but every few seconds her hands itch for her phone, that and the glass of wine she has already started drinking. She sees me looking and offers me one – with a wink. She says she shouldn't really drink she's trying for a baby. I lie and say – me too! And we clasp hands, just like that over the brochures as if we are trying together. I tell her all about my imaginary boyfriend who works in the city and we are having a nice time until I realise she is not going to offer me another glass...

It was nice...

At work Barry is back from Brussels and says I have a new glow and am I finally fucking someone. I tell him I have a girlfriend, his face, his little-boy face – so confused, so lustful, so fucking jealous. He wanders off to the kitchen and comfort-eats a packet of Hobnobs.

I have a voice note – so I take it to the loo – because I really am taking the piss with how much non-work I am doing today. And whilst I actually piss, I listen to my stepmother – Cassie.

Cassie loves a voice note because she thinks it's more 'personal' – and it allows her to keep talking without any interruptions.

She reminds me that we are having 'afternoon tea' this weekend – and I can't help but roll my eyes because who the fuck has 'afternoon tea'.

Eventually I shuffle back into the office – where Barry looks at me –

like I'm a fucking lunatic... because that was that Alice woman on the phone – and why haven't I put that rich bitch's offer in – and my heart sinks, my breath goes funny – but he covered... he covered. And he put the offer in.

And okay...

That's okay

I'll get over it.

The offer is accepted. Of course it fucking is.

Alice is delighted. She squeals and hangs up – does an Insta Live for her followers – talks about being blessed – time for #NewAdventures.

Then rings me back – unaware that I have just watched her – like two hundred and fifty-nine other strangers did – scream into the camera –

So what happens next?

We celebrate, I joke... but she says – *just like send me the deets. Thank you sooooo much you are such an angel.*

Barry tells me to send it to legal and they can go from there…

It was nice whilst it lasted it was nice whilst it lasted it was nice whilst it…

Tea with Cassie

The weekend arrives like it always does and I aim to sleep for most of it, sometimes I take three sleeping pills and just knock myself out...

But then I remember – Cassie. Shit. I get dressed from the corner of clothes in my room and spend the journey flattening down the creases over and over and over and –

My dad married Cassie a few years ago – the daughter of a family friend – two years above me at school, we would all go to France together when we were little and jump in waves... there was scandal and heartbreak and lots of interventions – but then everyone got over it and here they are – happy, living in a converted school in Norfolk making their own bread. They have twins called Petal and Pru. I am not fucking kidding, not even an ounce.

The café is *Alice in Wonderland*-themed because Cassie likes shit like that – wasn't he an actual paedophile, I say – and she covers the toddlers' ears – shhhhh – seriously... why would you say that? But she looks a bit embarrassed about the fact that she's worn a hairband in attempt to match the theme...

Eventually she asks me how work is... and before I can even tell her – she tells me that she doesn't miss it. Not at all. Nope, she hated her city-slicker lifestyle – hated it – and then goes – but you love it don't you...
You love your work

You love it – which is good because you haven't got kids –

And I have a sudden urge to pour scalding hot tea into my lap so that I can leave –

My phone rings. Thank fuck –

He's died – the man, the um... the husband of the older couple... with the beautiful two-point-one-million-pound house who now live in France – well he's only fucking snuffed it in the middle of a French market. And the sale is off because the wife actually hates their gîte in the Dordogne and wants to be back home in Blighty – she actually says the word Blighty… and IT'S OFF – THE SALE IS OFF!

I thank God and then feel mean about the man so do a sort of cross of fingers and a spit on the ground for good luck.

Gotta go – work – I say as I grab my coat –
And she sighs as she stuffs another cream puff in her face and says – see, all that rushing around, that's so not my lifestyle any more. Wave goodbye to your big sister.
But I'm already out the door and I don't even look back.

'I'm pregnant...'

Alice's face is so snotty when she cries. Daniel says – couldn't you have told us about the sale over the phone. Alice scowls at him – *she's being nice Daniel; she's being a decent fucking person*. And I smile apologetically at Daniel, this budget David Gandy who I must admit is even better looking in real life than in the many, many pictures of him on her account, the ones where he makes gnocchi on the weekends and does press-ups in the garden and sometimes gives her piggybacks...

It's just... it would have been really perfect... what with the baby...

And I gasp – like I'm in a fucking Spanish soap opera. And I hug her – because that seems like an okay-ish thing to do. I promise her I will find her the perfect house.
And Alice looks at me through her teary eyes – *don't like tell anyone... about the baby yeah. It's bad luck.*
Of course not.

Daniel interjects that they've got to create some content about paella so I better you know... go away.

Right... yeah... congratulations...

I spend the night watching them make a really watery paella on YouTube Live. Under a false name I write – have you put weight on? – sure you haven't got some news for us all – winky face

Suddenly a rush of comments – agreeing with me, yeah you look a bit bigger – are you expecting... look at her tummy – total baby bump! I have started something. She takes to Insta immediately like it's a government announcement.

She looks pissed off in her baby-blue eyes. In the background Daniel makes a lot of noise cleaning up the paella: *okay so the news is out... like I did have a reveal planned but whatever... I'm pregnant...*

...

SadBitch11

Alice and I are on our sixth house viewing, this time a modern apartment complex in Queens Road Peckham. It's fucking cheap and new-build, but it has a balcony and a bar on the roof so you know... it's cool.
Alice is trying to get the angles right for her selfies whilst stroking the perfectly little bump that is now showing – but the light is too harsh. She asks me how my pregnancy journey is going – which is rare as Alice doesn't really do questions – I mumble something about it not working out...

And suddenly we are in a trendy bar with too-loud music and very high chairs – and I am being petted by her, and so I say yeah and he left me – because neither of us can remember what name I gave my pretend boyfriend... and she even lets herself have a very large glass of wine with me – and I realise how desperate she has been because she sips it like it's spun sugar – And whilst she drinks it I secretly take a photo of her – so I can put it online later and say I was out with a friend.

When she orders just 'one more glass' – that's when I notice the tremor in her hands, and I know that something is wrong, that we are not here for me but for her – how are you Alice?

And she shows me this website – tittle.org. – and I know of forums, I am addicted to the Sidebar of Shame – I still bother with Facebook. But this... this is fucking insane.
This is Mumsnet on acid.
This is a website dedicated to any fucking weirdo who wants to spend pages and pages ranting about whichever Instagram influencer they hate most at the moment... it's incredible.
– Some bitch thinks Alice only got pregnant for the likes –
How sick is that – like it will increase her ad revenue but that's just me being honest...
And like she did want a baby...
One thread has seven thousand likes, four hundred and ninety-eight replies...

Seven thousand, four hundred and ninety-eight people are talking about Alice.

It's like bullying
But I don't care
They're just a bunch of sad fucks

Yeah… so sad…

Urgh it's just so nice to talk to someone old *like you who doesn't know about this shit –*

And I smile as I choke on my Pinot. Here to help…
Alice cycles home.

I sign in to tittle.org, I am SadBitch11 (that's right, eleven, because ten other people had that name already) and I lap it up greedily as people take the piss out of Alice, of Daniel, of their shitty life and their shitty faces…

…

I am a fucking god

And then it's another weekend and the pigeons are back at it.
On my phone Alice is endorsing a new yoga studio opened by
her friend Izzi – that's @IzziBeeBright on Instagram – who has
one-point-three million followers, which is way more than
Alice, although since Alice's announcement about the baby her
Instagram has gone mental as her brand domain has increased,
she is set to become a mumfluencer. *But a cool one*, she keeps
reminding me… with a twinge in her face. *I'll still be really
fucking cool…*

So I buy a pair of Lululemon leggings that are so expensive
I blush as I hand my card over and the woman behind the
counter sees – and says 'are you sure' – so I buy two.

The yoga studio is in Brixton, of course it is – in one of the
arches that used to be an Afro hair salon, but which now has
Izzi's handle graffitied across it by a #LocalArtist.

Alice actually smiles when she sees me – *OMG matching
leggings babe. You go girl* she says and almost high-fives me,
but she sees my hands are sweaty – she never sweats.

Her hair is in this messy bun piled on the top of her head and
I want to eat it.

And then Izzi swoops in on her – this tiny freckled thing – so
tiny and flexible you want to snip a tendon, really hobble the
bitch – and Alice gives her this big hug back and like girls at
school they squeal at each other and use 'babe' so many times
I can't actually keep up and during the class I make noises and
no one else does and at the end Izzi says, I don't know if
ashtanga is your thing babe. You have to find your own path
you know… just being honest. Jai.

I feel like a kid in PE again, told that I'm too shit to be in any
other position but goal, picking scabs on my knees to stop from
crying and crying and crying –
So I sign back in to tittle.org – SadBitch11 – and instead of just
liking and reading – this time I post: Alice and Izzi – best

friends? More like frenemies. And I tell them that Izzi secretly hates Alice for getting pregnant – that she is a fake and a fraud and her yoga class was fucking shit. And they go wild for it – the comments climb and climb – Because it turns out that people really, really love to hate other people, so I keep going – chatting shit about Daniel and Alice – about her clothes and her face and her shoes and her fucking car and her fucking pizza oven and as soon as I post something – someone – somewhere – replies in seconds and they keep wanting more and more and I feel like magic so I keep posting and all these sad fucks at home in Essex or Kent or wherever the fuck they live can't believe that I know them for real but I do – I fucking do – and I have the photos to prove it – I literally have a front-row fucking seat bitches and just like that – I AM A FUCKING GOD!

And I want Alice immediately.
To suffer something unfortunate.
To be friends with me
I don't know
Both...

Gorgon women

It's Monday – at work Barry says I have a spring in my step –
must be all the scissoring and I look at him confused until
I remember that I told him I had a girlfriend and he puts his
fingers together to try and mimic scissoring but he gets it wrong
and ends up doing that wiggly worm thing you do as a kid…
I nod, yeah I'm really happy. Good you miserable bitch…

And I am happy actually because on Tittle a woman called
Melissa has invited me to a private message board – she is the
queen bee and I have been chosen. Melissa and the sad fucks
are lapping me up, and every day they want more and more, a
new spill, some more tea and the monster is so very large and so
very hungry. They don't seem to need sleep.
Finally I have found my people.

Months pass and I show Alice a semi in Catford, a manor in
Crofton Park and a swish penthouse in Bermondsey and watch
as her bump gets bigger and bigger and her ankles start to puff a
little, spilling over the sides of her limited-edition Birkenstocks.
But she doesn't like any of them. Shame, I sigh – we'll just
have to keep looking.

Sometimes Cassie texts me asking if I want to do a pottery
course. But I just type back 'work' nothing else just 'work'.

…

The house Alice and Daniel finally decide on after all the
searching, surveys and rising damp – is an architectural wet
dream. I got them a reduced price, turns out Alice isn't as rich
as she looks, and Daniel's protein-bar sponsors don't actually
pay him yet. It even has a massive fuck-off garden – no rose
bushes though. Alice is delighted – she needs another project,
now she can add 'garden guru' to her Insta profile.

The contracts are signed, the keys are being exchanged this
Friday. It's been months. *And you've been our rock*, she says,
our good-luck charm. And Daniel smirks, and as he walks me to

the door – he says – nice knowing you – thanks – and he closes it before I even have the chance to say... no problem...

And suddenly I am crying. I am crying hot salty angry tears so hard and big and fast I feel like I could drown and I don't know how or why but suddenly I'm in an All Bar One...
In central London?
How did I get here? Did I walk? I'm on my second bottle of acidic Pinot and there is a hen party in the corner, gorgon women with sashes and glitter and penis straws all over the table next to plates of creamy carbonara and the pop pop of Prosecco echoes round the ceilings. And in the toilet as I put more and more make-up on my tear-stained face I notice that one of them has left a sash on the counter... so I put it on and I join them and no one bats an eyelid, because most of their eyes are in the backs of their heads –
And the mother of the bride tells me I am a good girl and before I know it we are singing karaoke in a bar round the corner and a man buys us all a round of cheap shots until he's told to fuck off and the bride is screaming at her best mate about how she fucking hates her – hates her but now they're hugging and we're all singing along to 'if you wannabe my lover' and there is a pile of regurgitated carbonara behind the velvet sofa and...

I sit on the night bus home and I look at Alice... she has posted a picture of keys – #NewHome #Blessed. But she doesn't thank me. I try to message the WhatsApp group with drunk fingers but it's just a string of emojis... and no one answers. How could they... I've not said anything.

Bumpdate

Now that there is no Alice to show around the houses of South London I start to deflate a little, like a balloon… rubbery and used. The Tittle lot are bored of me – nothing new to add, no photos to upload, no inside scoop, my posts slip in the rankings, Melissa asks if I've lost my touch. Someone says I was making it all up all along. That I never actually knew her…

Alice on the other hand is on fire on Instagram,
Embracing this crazy pregnancy journey the only way I know how #Chocolate #Ad

She's been endorsed by a new maternity outfitter now that she's ready to fucking burst

BUMPDATE – Gotta do pregnancy in style ladies –

and she's all sparkly dungarees with really low fucking awful crotches and rainbow-patterned Uggs and frankly she looks like a unicorn shitting glitter, but people are lapping it up.

On tittle.org I start a thread about her shitty DIY videos and how Daniel never seems to be at any of the baby scans, and has anyone else noticed how Alice's acne is back? But people don't comment as much as usual – they've heard it all before…
And Alice doesn't rise to the bait – not once… she just keeps painting the walls petal pink and monsoon orange.

So on Sunday I make sure to be at the trendy market she mentioned on that podcast last week – you know the one with the chorizo stall and the five-pound Cronut stand.
And I see her – she's with Daniel – and they're walking ever so slightly apart like they've argued and I wave – and Daniel tries to steer her away but too late motherfucker because
Oh hi! Hi
And he excuses himself to go and look at some handmade razors and we stand there just staring at each other and she is stroking her perfectly round, perfectly massive bump and I realise
I should say something like 'wow look at you' so I do and she smiles because she's pleased and I reach out and I touch it.

And she flinches a little because these days you're meant to
ask…
And I keep my hand there
Hard.
And she backs up

I felt it kick…
I lie and it's the worst lie because she, she of all people in the
entire universe knows that it didn't.

She points at my tote bag and says *what are you here for*…
And… er… dinner party…
And she says *yeah we're stocking up for the house-warming*…

And then Daniel swoops in and says they need to go and he puts
his hand so firmly on her back and steers her away and just
before they're gone, she turns around and says – *you should
come – next Saturday. To the party. To the house-warming*…

And I forgot to take a photo… for Tittle… for me…

…

The party

Saturday. The house-warming. I am clutching a bottle of not-too-cheap wine and wearing a brand-new dress I bought especially. I have on double-strength deodorant and have been chewing gum all day and I think I look... nice?
Their front door has been painted a powdery blue, periwinkle? He opens it – Daniel – and oh... you came? Daniel curls his lip in that way of his, takes the wine like it's a leaky bag of dogshit and retreats into the corridor.

There are people everywhere wearing jeans and T-shirts and I'm wearing heels and no one else is. There are balloons – the big crinkly foil ones, that look shit in real life but really good on Instagram and fairy lights and a photo booth and isn't that fun and all around the house – the house that I sold them – are tiny shelves with even tinier succulents on them and neon signs that say things like 'love' and 'lol' and in the kitchen there is a baby-blue AGA and up the stairs is the wallpaper that costs so much it makes my heart hurt and in the master bedroom there is nothing on his side of the bed but an empty tub of protein powder...

And in the baby's room...

In the baby's room the walls are painted petal pink and monsoon orange and the whole thing is so beautiful and all the new baby clothes are lined up in a neat little row #Gifted and there is the mobile hanging above the designer cot – which I had commented looked like a murder of crows and she'd replied – *no silly it's blackbirds like in the nursery rhyme...* and I wanted to snatch the whole thing down...
I sit there on the soft, soft carpet and breathe it in and it feels like maybe I could lock the doors and just live here, in this house. In this room –

And then I hear her – Alice – her laugh floats up through the open window and I look outside and there – there she is

So I follow the sound of her laugh to the back of the garden when suddenly I hear him... Daniel –

That fuckin' estate-agent woman is here again – and Alice sighs
– *I was being polite*.

I get closer and closer – hidden behind the newly planted rose
bushes – but I can see them.
They're standing there all huddled in a group – Daniel and
Alice and Izzi – who is chain-smoking which would be fucking
carnage if anyone on Insta found out.
And Izzi sniffs – is that the weird one who came to my class?
Alice nods – *yeah, she's just a bit… sad*.
And Daniel curls his lip once again and says – Sad! If she was a
dog she would be put down.

Daniel! Alice cries but then laughs. Really laughs. *You're so
mean*. But she smiles as she says it.

And they walk back up to the house which is lit up like a big
birthday cake in a fairy tale, and as they do they pass me and
Alice says – *Babe! so glad you could make it*.
And squeezes my cold fat arm.

And I grab my phone out of my shitty clutch purse and I sign in.
SadBitch11, that's me. And I don't even think I just do it…
I post a photo of Alice
The one from the bar
High chairs
Too-loud music
Multiple glasses of wine
Spun sugar
Baby bump just visible
and underneath I write:
Pretty sure you're not mean to down Pinot when pregnant.
DONE.

…

I don't know you?

It takes two days for Alice to lose all her sponsors, they all argue that it's not about the wine – they're not judging, no judgement obviously – just conflicting schedules...

And I should be smiling... shouldn't I ... because the outrage is huge and Tittle are practically worshipping at my feet, the story runs in all the online mags, the blogs, and it's trending on all the platforms. Right now they're talking about Alice on *Loose Women*... and she's not posted anything for twenty-four hours and that's social-media suicide... she might as well just be dead.

And it's everything I ever wanted –

But I don't... I don't smile once.

The next few days, instead of everyone talking about something or someone else, it grows, people are telling Alice on Twitter that she should go and kill herself, that some women shouldn't be allowed ovaries – forced sterilisation – that she should just fucking shoot herself in the fucking face.
It doesn't stop, none of it stops and I read every single fucking comment. Until I can't breathe with it.

I text Alice asking if she is okay... no reply... until... the little dots.
The silence –
The little dots –
She says she's *really, really tired*.
The little dots –
The silence –
The little dots –
She says I should *come round*.
Come round.
Now.
Just like that.
I tell her I'M ON MY WAY.
And I finish the bottle of wine I was drinking and start walking.
Even though she lives fucking miles away.

And I can tell they've had an argument the moment I step on their lovely little home doormat, because the silence is painful

I'm here – I smile and she doesn't –
In fact Alice is looking for the first time... a bit mad... stuck rabbit and Daniel looms over the banister at me like a fucked-up Cheshire Cat.
We wanted to talk to you –

And I realise then – that I have walked into a trap.

I'm handling it actually Daniel
And Alice twists her pouty little face and she screws up her eyes and says
We know it was you
The post – the photo, it was you
That bar in Peckham

And of course she remembers the bar, too-high chairs, loud music and that means every single post –

Was –
SadBitch11 – at least you know what you are *mate* Daniel spits.

And Alice keeps twisting and turning her face a blotchy purple I've not seen before
And she says in this whiny voice so hard and high and thin –
You've ruined my life
And like – you don't even fucking know me.

I don't know you?

I don't know you – I'm laughing now. Fucking hysterical –

I know everything about you, you stupid cunt – it's all here on your page, your videos, your posts, your pictures, your channel, your hashtags – what you wear and eat and drink and the way you wrinkle your nose and don't like artichokes and get sick if you eat gluten, the linen on your bed, the type of pants you wear, the way you loooove peanut butter on bananas because you did a whole fucking thing about it – which isn't fucking cooking by the way – the amount of times you exercise a day, the way you brush your hair, what shampoo you use, the way

you rub coconut oil into your belly and your stretch marks but
how you also tell people not to care about their stretch marks.
How you are so scared of having a baby but want a baby but
also felt like you just had to have one because of the fucking
content it would generate – I know everything about you,
because you want me to – so do not – do not fucking tell me
I shouldn't, that I don't... because you fucking invited me in.
You fucking pressed follow.

And they threaten to call the police.

So I leave...

...

On the way home I check my socials – I've been blocked.
I've been blocked by Alice on everything.

Her number won't connect and I... I...

I cry so hard on the way home that I feel like crawling. So
I do... I crawl.

...

Too big. Too small

The pigeons have gone. I stopped putting bread out for them so
they fucked off.
I saw a dead one by the side of the road… and I thought, did
I kill it…

Crushed wings and small bones by the bins.

Alice tells her followers about me – about SadBitch11.
Tittle goes wild.

Now that my identity has been revealed people are quick to
shun me. Everyone has decided that Alice is the real victim. The
tide has turned so very quickly. It's now my turn on the merry-
go-round of shitty comments, how can I be so cruel, why don't
I just curl up and fucking die #BeKind.

Melissa tries to stand up for me bless her – she's found religion
recently and likes preaching forgiveness –
she sends me memes of God in the clouds and rainbows – the
presence of an almighty
She says she has been there and understands
Understands the ball of pain inside
The hollow, the squeeze
The lethargy, the hatred
The numb
The numb
The numb
I send her clips of very intense and very illegal porn until she
stops completely.

Barry keeps calling – I haven't turned up for work – again –
what the fuck is going on. I put my phone on silent.

I'm busy having to make loads of new fake accounts to follow
Alice now that her profile is private – when I see it –
A shot of them in the car – Daniel driving, brand-new baby seat
in the back #Ad and the caption underneath #ItsTime…
#AreYouReady?

And I think no…
You are so not ready for this.
But I am.

…

King's College Hospital they said would be the place – because even though she wanted a home birth obvs and a water birth obvs, she also wanted a shit ton of drugs – obvs.

I get on the bus and I make a beep noise because my Oyster is dead but the gleam in my eyes tells the driver just to let me on. And I sit there all cosy and warm and the wheels on the bus go round and round and I remember singing that song so many times as a kid until my mum smacked the back of my legs with her umbrella and told me to stop.

Told me to just stop already…

To just stop –

I can't stop now –

And I see it – the big hospital –

And I run in – get into the lift and maternity maternity – level six –
And there is a white rabbit who guides the way because even they have gone with an *Alice in Wonderland* theme and I have to stop myself from screaming PAEDO PAEDO as I run through the corridors and I'm late, I'm late, I'm going to be late

Because the baby could already be here saying hello to the world and I need to help Alice.

So I peek through windows and doors at hands and boobs and babies and little cots and busy women and men rushing around, and blood slicks on the floor and cries and moans and this smell of sickly almonds.

And there she is… sleeping just look at her face and her eyes and her little hands all bundled up

She's so fast asleep

Shhh... Don't make a sound...

Tiny little face

I could just reach down

And pick her up
And take her home couldn't I...

I could do anything to her

Couldn't I

Too big
Too small
Eat me

Alice.

Just sleeping – looks exhausted, looks frankly pretty shitty if
you ask me, life bleached out of her –
And his jacket is on the chair – so he's here somewhere

And where is she... eh...
Where is the bouncing baby girl?...

And she's been crying
Still is
Little sobs

The floor is slick with bleach

And the light keeps flickering or am I imagining it – that
whining noise.

And I lean over her

Her sad little face

Alice's howling mouth

And I take my fist and I think about smashing it hard into her
skull.

But instead I crawl in next to her and hold her

Alice

Because she's sad and overwhelmed

And

For a second she gives in
And she holds me back and I think she knows it's me… maybe
even murmurs my name

And it's just bliss

And there is no little baby in the room

Because there is no little baby

It didn't… it didn't work out…

Stillborn.

And I can't help but remember the pigeon – the wind knocked
out of it, dead little thing –

And I keep thinking – everyone on Instagram will be so
disappointed

I stroke her hair

and I tell her it's all alright… it's all right.

And I tell her a story… all about how I met a girl called Alice
And how all hell broke loose in that little room on the top floor
of the broken hospital on that shiny hill on that rainy night…

New adventures

Work let me go – I haven't been myself recently they say. Barry helps me pack my things into a box he borrows from the Chinese takeaway next door. Everything smells of prawn crackers.

He pushes me up against the door of my flat and tries for a goodbye snog. But I just shake my head and say I'm on my period – actual clumps and that seems to put him off – in the end he gives me twenty quid and tells me to look after myself. Which is nice I suppose.

I sit in my flat and I am alone.
I sleep for a week and this time I don't need to take any sleeping pills…

No one has said anything on Tittle about the baby – I left the site – Melissa sent me one more message – telling me to see someone, that I need help clearly. And I felt like screaming – of course I need help Melissa – so does everyone. But I didn't press send. I just left it hanging in the internet.

There are sharp pains in my arms and my chest and my heart.
I google pains
Pain
I feel pain
All the time
And get the lyrics of a shitty emo song.
It's terrible but I listen to it thirty-five times
And then become a fan on Facebook
And then delete my account because I've ruined it.

Cassie notices this and asks if I'm okay – she wanted to invite me to stay actually – Dad is doing a cycling holiday in New Zealand with the local bike club who are all much younger and much more female than him… so there's loads of space, tons of it in fact in the converted school… it's a bit spooky she whimpers… and then laughs – silly me.
I hang up.

I hang up.
I hang up.

And then the doorbell rings – the actual doorbell and I'd
forgotten what it sounded like so it makes me jump and I run to
the door –

It's my landlady – and she's got a couple who are thinking of
buying the flat – can they come in – she did email

And I *laugh* hard because this is usually my job – showing
shiny stupid fucking couples round a flat they can't really
afford.

Sure come in I say and I am proud of the fact that it smells so
bad, and I don't even bother to hide the used tampon with my
foot or anything and he even mutters 'God' as he enters –
I point out all the features, I say here is my mould collection,
and this here is the broken dishwasher and this – this is a plant
that decided to grow through the windowsill from the outside
which I think you'll find is very in right now. Oh and here's
where the pigeons no longer live.

But he's clever – he eyes me up and says we'll take it and I
think fuck – well done you – because actually this flat is
fucking cheap for this area… it's up-and-coming don't you
know – transport links et cetera et cetera…

And that's that.

So I pack my shit into bin bags which I dump up and down the
street – because who needs it really and I have no plan and no
clue and nowhere to go and…

Just like that I'm outside the periwinkle-blue door and it looks
so dark and quiet. The rose bushes have grown wild and saggy.
The bins are overflowing and there are clothes hangers spilling
out and into the road –

They must be having a clear-out… the baby's room… maybe

Her Instagram is silent these days, her Twitter deleted, her
YouTube dormant. She's disappeared. Like she never existed.
Like she was never even real.

I walk up to the front door and I'm sweating so hard, I just want to say sorry and maybe maybe she will forgive me and we can start again maybe.

Alice.

Because I don't want her to suffer
And I think we could be friends
Maybe
Eventually
And I knock
Coming she shouts
And I can hear her feet padding down the stairs
And my breath is so –
She's coming down the corridor
Wooden floors
And she's opening the door

And it's Alice…

Beautiful tear-stained Alice and there's blood dripping down her JoJo Maman blouse and her really expensive leggings and she tells me that she smacked her face against the baby-blue AGA – just so she could feel something because she gets it – she gets why I did it –

And I put my hand up to her face

And it's not Alice.

Hello
I'm Laura – the estate agent – are you here for the viewing?

And I turn around and see it now, proper, the sign behind the overgrown rose bush –

For Sale.

And inside the house is empty – because
She's already gone.
#NewAdventures

And I lie and nod and she shows me round the beautiful empty sad sad house – with the barely used blue AGA and the broken

neon lights. I sit in the baby's room and the murder of crows…
no, blackbirds… stare back at me and –
And I have to make my excuses and leave
Because another woman appears at the door and Hello sorry to
interrupt –
I'm here for the viewing?

And I am out of there…
And I breathe this weird animal sob in my throat and my face

And I ring her – Cassie – because I would like to stay if that's
still possible and she says yes – I… I am so lonely here.

And I get there – and she's waiting in the doorway with the
twins clutching at her legs – fuck – they're walking now.

And they have buckets and spades and we go to the beach just
before the sun sets
And at one point
Cassie grabs my hand and we jump through the waves.

And I wonder then if being friends with me doesn't mean you
need to suffer something unfortunate.
That I am not that unfortunate thing you need to suffer
That I am not unfortunate
Or suffering.
Both…
I don't know.

End.

A Nick Hern Book

Harm first published in Great Britain in 2021 as a paperback original by Nick Hern Books Limited, The Glasshouse, 49a Goldhawk Road, London W12 8QP, in association with the Bush Theatre, London

Harm copyright © 2021 Phoebe Eclair-Powell

Phoebe Eclair-Powell has asserted her moral right to be identified as the author of this work

Cover photo of Kelly Gough: Art direction by Doug Kerr, Photography by Laurie Fletcher

Designed and typeset by Nick Hern Books, London
Printed in the UK by Mimeo Ltd, Huntingdon, Cambridgeshire PE29 6XX

A CIP catalogue record for this book is available from the British Library

ISBN 978 1 84842 993 2